EAT L:
BOOK SE

C000137049

Eat Like a Local- Sara........ ... .
Guide

I have lived in the Sarasota area since 1998 and learned about many great places that I want to try. –Conoal

EAT LIKE A LOCAL-CONNECTICUT: Connecticut Food Guide

This a great guide to try different places in Connecticut to eat. Can't wait to try them all! The author is awesome to explore and try all these different foods/drinks. There are places I didn't know they existed until I got this book and I am a CT resident myself! –Caroline J. H.

EAT LIKE A LOCAL- LAS VEGAS: Las Vegas Nevada Food Guide

Perfect food guide for any tourist traveling to Vegas or any local looking to go outside their comfort zone! –TheBondes

Eat Like a Local-Jacksonville: Jacksonville Florida Food Guide

Loved the recommendations. Great book from someone who knows their way around Jacksonville. –Anonymous

EAT LIKE A LOCAL- COSTA BRAVA: Costa Brava Spain Food Guide

The book was very well written. Visited a few of the restaurants in the book, they were great! Sylvia V.

Eat Like a Local-Sacramento: Sacramento California Food Guide

As a native of Sacramento, Emerald's book touches on some of our areas premier spots for food and fun. She skims the surface of what Sacramento has to offer recommending locations in historical, popular areas where even more jewels can be found. –Katherine G.

EAT LIKE A LOCAL- MEXICO CITY

Mexico City Food Guide

Paulina Armendáriz

CZYK Publishing Since 2011.
CZYKPublishing.com
Eat Like a Local

Lock Haven, PA
All rights reserved.
ISBN: 9798518998469

BOOK DESCRIPTION

Are you excited about planning your next trip? Do you want an edible experience? Would you like some culinary guidance from a local? If you answered yes to any of these questions, then this Eat Like a Local book is for you. Eat Like a Local- Mexico by Author Paulina Armendáriz wants you to skip the tacos (sort of) and try some different local Mexican food. A Culinary tourism is an important aspect of any travel experience. Food has the ability to tell you a story of a destination, its landscapes, and culture on a single plate. Most food guides tell you how to eat like a tourist. Although there is nothing wrong with that, as part of the Eat Like a Local series, this book will give you a food guide from someone who has lived at your next culinary destination.

In these pages, you will discover advice on having a unique edible experience. This book will not tell you exact addresses or hours but instead will give you excitement and knowledge of food and drinks from a local that you may not find in other travel food guides.

Eat like a local. Slow down, stay in one place, and get to know the food, people, and culture. By the time you finish this book, you will be eager and prepared to travel to your next culinary destination.

OUR STORY

Traveling has always been a passion of the creator of the Eat Like a Local book series. During Lisa's travels in Malta, instead of tasting what the city offered, she ate at a large fast-food chain. However, she realized that her traveling experience would have been more fulfilling if she had experienced the best of local cuisines. Most would agree that food is one of the most important aspects of a culture. Through her travels, Lisa learned how much locals had to share with tourists, especially about food. Lisa created the Eat Like a Local book series to help connect people with locals which she discovered is a topic that locals are very passionate about sharing. So please join me and: Eat, drink, and explore like a local.

TABLE OF CONTENTS

DEDICATION

To my two great loves.

My grandma, who has always shared her love with me through food.

My husband, who welcomed me into his city and heart.

ABOUT THE AUTHOR

Paulina is a trained chef, food and travel writer, and Mexican entrepreneur. Having grown up in China, she was brought up with a sense of wonder for new cultures, politics, and most importantly, food. Over time, sichuan peppercorns and shaoxing wine became flavors more well known to her than those back home. That was never an issue though, because she's always considered herself to be from everywhere she's ever lived.

When she was not in China, she was in Texas helping out in her grandma's restaurant from the age of four. Being surrounded by food, different flavors and textures always intrigued her but she never really explored the kitchen herself until she was nineteen. Moving to a different city and lots of burnt rice after, she realized food was her true passion and enrolled in culinary school. She has since graduated with a degree in Gastronomy and Culinary Arts and opened up her own bakery in Mexico City.

Paulina now spends her days writing and running her own kitchen, *Pizquita de Azúcar*. At Pizquita de Azúcar, she strives to make the best products using fresh fruit and change the concept of sweet desserts. With the help of her self-proclaimed quality control inspector and husband, she's always whipping up magical desserts. Hoping to expand soon into the restaurant business with a fusion of Mexican and Chinese food, desserts are just the beginning!

HOW TO USE THIS BOOK

The goal of this book is to help culinary travelers either dream or experience different edible experiences by providing opinions from a local. The author has made suggestions based on their own knowledge. Please do your own research before traveling to the area in case the suggested locations are unavailable.

Travel Advisories: As a first step in planning any trip abroad, check the Travel Advisories for your intended destination.
https://travel.state.gov/content/travel/en/traveladvisories/traveladvisories.html

FROM THE PUBLISHER

Traveling can be one of the most important parts of a person's life. The anticipation and memories that you have are some of the best. As a publisher of the *Eat Like a Local*, Greater Than a Tourist, as well as the popular *50 Things to Know* book series, we strive to help you learn about new places, spark your imagination, and inspire you. Wherever you are and whatever you do I wish you safe, fun, and inspiring travel.

Lisa Rusczyk Ed. D.
CZYK Publishing

There is a popular saying in Mexico that goes *"donde come uno, comen dos"*, which means there's always room for one more at the table. To me, this encompasses just how warm and welcoming our culture is. No Mexican mom or *abuela* (granny) has ever made just enough food for every family member to help themselves once. No. We like to cook in big batches so there are always leftovers. Who will eat them? Perhaps the hungry sister or an unexpected guest.

While we do not invite strangers into our homes, Mexicans enjoy having company and sharing a meal over pretty much any form of entertainment. It's also a tradition that different budgets can afford. Regardless of whether you're sharing steak and guacamole at the weekend *carne asada* (barbecue) or some refried beans and scrambled eggs, the same spirit of giving and joy is present. We don't always plan to have people over, but our homes and hearts are always open to those we love.

Thus, if you're invited into someone's home, you're being welcomed into so much more. Their lives, their history, and secret recipes. Because let's face it, no one would share a bite of granny's secret recipe with someone they don't like. So if you're lucky to find yourself inside a Mexican home, be thankful, and most importantly, express how much you like the food.

Food is a huge part of our culture. In fact, I don't think there is a single gathering in which food isn't part of the reason for the get-together, planned or otherwise. If you're watching a football game with friends, you can expect there to be food. If you're just catching up with someone, you can expect there to be food. Having no reason in particular to get together is also a reason enough to. And yes, you can expect food there too. Sometimes it's potlucks and other times it's just store-bought pizza, but food is a major requirement. You're never obligated to bring something but trust me when I tell you that opening the door to a friend bearing gifts (potato chips or anything edible) has never been met with anything other than extreme gratitude. More food is an excuse for a longer gathering.

Everything that's brought over is placed on the table, and the minute you set it down, someone will be leaning over to see what it is and open it. It's almost like Christmas morning, except the only gifts are food. Even if you bring a bag of chips, food is food. It's part of the glue that holds our society together and it's how we continue to shape our traditions and create new ones.

While restaurants do not take our saying "*donde come uno, comen dos*" quite literally, otherwise they'd go broke, the food follows the same principle. It's warm and welcoming. It's rich and tells a story. It tells our story, so I hope you're ready to listen because we've already made room for you at our table.

Mexico City
Mexico

Mexico City
Mexico
Climate

	High	Low
January	72	41
February	75	43
March	79	46
April	80	50
May	81	53
June	78	55
July	76	54
August	76	54
September	75	53
October	75	49
November	74	45
December	73	42

GreaterThanaTourist.com

Temperatures are in Fahrenheit degrees.
Source: NOAA

1. HERE'S TO CANTINAS

Cantinas have been an important aspect of Mexican culture since the days of the Revolution when men showed up for their daily fill and hearty meal. Despite cantinas being known for cheap drinks, the food was the real jewel. Inexpensive, simple, but extremely delicious, *cantina* foods like *chamorros* and tacos quickly became a staple for the average Joe's diet.

Today, you won't precisely find a Pancho Villa in the every-day *cantina* or be a spectator to a war rally, but the vibe is still there, especially in those found in Coyoacán. While not all cantinas are created equal, I would dare say the ones in this part of town are certainly the most authentic. Plus, there's one for every budget, which is always nice to know when you're travelling! So let's start with the most budget-friendly and work our way up:

- Centenario 107
- La Calaca
- La Coyoacana
- La Veinte

While most of these offer service throughout the whole day, I would recommend dedicating a big chunk of the day to exploring Coyoacán. The area is

13

also known for its history, beautiful colonial architecture, markets, fountains and kiosks. The word "Coyoacán" means Palace of Coyotes in Náhuatl, an indigenous language. Thankfully, you will not find any of these creatures roaming around freely but you can certainly spot a couple in the commemorative fountains. Don't worry, they haven't bitten anyone in several decades!

2. PASS THE CORN

All of this walking around in Coyoacán is a little tiring though, so I recommend loading up on some *esquites*. Esquites are corn ears served hot with a bit of cream or mayo, cheese, chili, and a little bit of lemon. You can also get the corn on the cob and have it prepared the same way, so to each their own! Either way, they are a popular snack and the ones in Coyoacán have garnered fame for being the best ones so I highly recommend them.

The *puestitos* (street-food stalls) start appearing around 5:00 PM on weekdays and 3:00 PM on weekends, so if you're around make sure to get some! However, I do not recommend stopping for some on your way to a restaurant or cantina. They aren't exactly a light snack and will have you sitting with a full belly while others enjoy a delicious meal. It's not the first time this has happened to me, and it probably won't be my last (they are that good!) - but you have been warned.

3. IT TAKES TWO TO MANGO

Speaking of snacks, you cannot miss the *fruta con chile.* This snack basically translates to fruit with chili powder. It is amazing and extremely refreshing, so if you're visiting during the hotter months of the year, make sure to grab a cup of your favorite fruit with a dash of chili powder. Popular varieties include jicama, mango, and coconut.

You can algo get it with all sorts of spicy sauces and powders. A must-try is definitely *chamoy*, a tangy apricot-based sauce. If you can take the heat from the mixture, you might just love them enough to take some home with you! Not the fruit, the sauces!

4. FLAMING HOT CHEETOS' MUSE

Papitas preparadas are potato chips that have been prepared with several sauces (some of them are spicy so make sure to ask before you agree to everything!) and lemon. Mexicans take their chips very seriously so make sure to grab some while you're out and about.

For those of you that really want to know what you might be getting yourselves into, I can tell you this much: explosions of flavor and texture. The potato chips are usually much thicker and crunchier than Lays, and they are also huge (which is awesome if you love chips). The lemon and combination of sauces added to them are just amazing, so make sure to get them all! Beware, though, Mexicans love spicy sauces so always ask which one is which and don't go heavy on the hot sauce if you can't take that much of it. Some carts even offer additional toppings on your chips like peanuts and *rielitos* (small tamarind candies that look like Hot Tamales candy).

5. CEVICHE THAT WON'T MAKE YOU CRABBY

Now, so as not to wander too far from the freshness of prepared fruit, I will leave a plate of *ceviche* and slowly walk away… Ceviche is originally a Peruvian dish that Mexicans took into their own hands several decades ago. The result was all kinds of fresh and crunchy variations. A typical ceviche consists of raw seafood cured in lemon juice, with chopped onion, tomato, chili, and coriander. While seemingly simple, the flavors are surprising!

To start off, go for the simple ones so you have something to compare the rest to. In my opinion, the best ceviches are the simplest ones, made from fish or shrimp, but that does not mean more exotic ones aren't worth it. In fact, some of my favorite ceviches have habanero, coconut and even strawberry, so don't be afraid to play around!

Unfortunately, Mexico City is not a coastal city so fresh fish isn't exactly an everyday thing. However, don't let this dishearten you! The city is not too far from Acapulco, one of the main ports in the country, so good seafood restaurants bring the fish over. Plus, you did not come to Mexico to eat defrosted fish. Luckily for you, I will not let you run astray in this culinary journey so I've gathered the best tried-and-true seafood restaurants/eateries so you won't have to. Here they are:

- Contramar
- Cabanna
- Los Arcos

6. SOMETHING SMELLS FISHY

In keeping with the seafood vibe, I will now discuss a type of taco that has divided the country: the fish taco. I know, I know... the title of this book says to skip the tacos, but this is one of the few exceptions to make. Now, to answer the real question... Yes, seafood tacos exist and they are amazing! The most popular ones are fish and several states dispute the original recipe. While none of them are originally from Mexico City, *chilangos* (people from Mexico City) have grown so fond of them they've found ways to make them their own.

Let's dive into it! The most famous fish tacos are from Ensenada in the state of Baja California. While this is nowhere near a day-trip from Mexico City, you can definitely enjoy them in different spots around the city. Ensenada-style fish tacos consist of light and crispy beer-battered fish in a corn tortilla, topped with shredded cabbage, mayonnaise and/or cream, some *pico de gallo* (a typical accompaniment made from chopped tomato, onion, and coriander), salsas and lemon juice to taste. So what exactly sets them apart from fish tacos in the rest of the country? Well, we have been debating this for a few decades and still can't put a finger on it. As a very humble but educated opinion, it has something to do with the way the batter is spiced and, I could almost swear this, the freshness of the fish. Other than that, I cannot fathom Baja California cultivating magical tomatoes and cabbage that taste a thousand times better than anywhere else.

Anyway, when you get your hands on some of these, make sure to get them with everything! The cabbage, pico de gallo, mayonnaise, and salsas all add flavorful and textural components to the taco. Do not miss out on anything! Even if you're not so sure of the flavor combination, the only thing you should be worried about is figuring out which is the spicy salsa. Especially if you're not so good with the heat, make sure to try a little bit first and then go from there. Baby steps, but here are two good places to get you started:

- Taco Fish
- El Pescadito

7. SHRIMPLY IRRESISTIBLE

Now, let's talk about the taco fit for a king (or a governor at least!). The beloved *taco gobernador* was allegedly invented in Mazatlán, in the state of Sinaloa, in 1987 when the then-governor visited a famous seafood restaurant. The chef wanted to impress him so much that he fusioned several of his favorite ingredients into one dish. Thus, the taco gobernador (which translates into 'The Governor Taco') made of shrimp, cheese, bell peppers, and *chile poblano*, was born. Whether the story is true or not is still a matter of heated debate, especially in Mazatlán, but the restaurant is still open and proudly calls itself the creator of the taco gobernador.

I don't care much whether it is true or not because, in my opinion, it is one of the best seafood restaurants around and has been since it opened. How can I be so sure? I spent every one of my birthdays there for around five years before moving abroad. My family was also a regular there, so much so that on my last birthday spent there the chef gifted me an embroidered apron to make me an official part of the crew. I wonder if I could pass for a waitress if I went in there wearing it?

Call me biased if you must, but I will set myself on fire if it isn't the best, or one of the best, seafood restaurants in town. By now, you must be on edge just waiting for me to shut up and tell you the name of the restaurant, so here it is: Los Arcos.

8. FROM GOVERNORS TO CARDINALS

If we've talked about food fit for a governor, why not the cardinal too? That's the name of our next restaurant! *El Cardenal* (The Cardinal) is a very famous traditional Mexican restaurant in Mexico City loved by young and old alike because of its delicious food and cozy atmosphere. El Cardenal evokes the sensation of a typical Saturday morning for the average Mexican family, with a warm homemade breakfast and some sweet bread.

The restaurant opened its doors in 1969 without any intent of world domination. In fact, it opened with the mere purpose of providing sustenance for the founding family. However, the flavors spoke for themselves and started conquering hearts right away. Today, El Cardenal is a family restaurant with several locations throughout Mexico

21

City, but if you really want to be blown away, visit the one in *San Ángel*, a picturesque district.

Although breakfast, lunch, and dinner are equally good, I have to recommend going for breakfast. Why? The freshly baked *conchas con nata* (sweet bread with a side of custard) and hot chocolate are to die for! Make sure to arrive early because they run out quickly. Even if you're not sure what you're going to have, order the conchas con nata first. Everything else can wait. I promise.

9. MEXICAN MCDONALD'S

Luckily for you, not all restaurants in the city (or all their dishes) are as highly demanded as the conchas con nata at El Cardenal. You can thank me later for this recommendation: *La Casa de Toño* (Toño's House). With more than fifty locations, you can be sure to run into this franchise practically anywhere. While it doesn't have nearly as many locations as an international fast food chain, La Casa de Toño is as close as you get to a Mexican McDonald's.

Don't get me wrong, you will not find any burgers at La Casa de Toño. No. This restaurant is the holy grail for Mexican *garnachas* (a term referring to street food made with *masa*, a corn dough). You can find *flautas, sopes,* and best of all: *pozole!* While all of these are matches made in heaven, I am going to go all out for the flautas and pozole at this place. Flautas are deep-fried tacos filled with just about anything. The most common ones are beef, chicken, and perhaps potato. They are served hot and topped with chopped lettuce, cream, and cheese. While they are amazing as they are, the salsas you can add are the cherries on top.

Red or green, don't underestimate these delicious salsas because they are not just red or green. Some red salsas are made from charred tomato and onion, while others are packed with a combination of dried red chilis. Green salsas are typically made from *tomatillo* (a small green tomato), green chilis and sometimes avocado. No two are alike. Ever. People love their salsas so much that waiters often bring small bowls of different ones to the table. We speak the language of salsas and know that one is never enough, we need them all.

Put some salsa on your forearm, near your wrist, and give it a try like any good Mexican before you generously pour it over your flautas. It would not be the first time someone has been innocently blindsided by a salsa, and those stories end in tears.

10. A SOUP FROM THE HEAVENS

Although we've gone over several dishes fit for political and religious leaders, the soup we will now discuss comes directly from the heavens. Pozole, a rich pork broth spiced with chilis and served with kernels, was originally offered to the Gods by the Aztecs. After a sacrifice was made, the person's body was used to make a soup that was then enjoyed by the rest of the community. I'm not much of a historian, but as much as I know the Aztecs used plenty of chili in their meals, I'm going to take a wild guess and say the redness of the soup also came from the blood. Luckily, that was long ago and we have since adjusted one or two ingredients because, you know… human sacrifice is no longer a thing?

With that out of the way (thankfully), we can return to the more normal and delicious aspects of pozole. The only other thing that comes close to it in terms of richness, in my opinion, is Japanese Tonkotsu ramen. While you may find different versions of it, the most popular is certainly pozole *rojo*. What does this look like? Well, it's red. The others are either green or clear, so you can't really go wrong with pozole if you know that what you're ordering should be red.

Now onto the toppings, pozole is typically topped with chopped lettuce, thin slices of radish, and a little bit of oregano. Some people even like to add bits of avocado. Mexicans still haven't reached a consensus on avocado in pozole yet, so I'll let you make up your own mind. However, I will say that the added creaminess from the avocado is both nice and diverting. It's nice because you get a little bit of sweetness, but that same sweetness also changes the flavor of the broth completely. I say try it with and without, and decide which one you like best!

Finally, a good place to have this dish is La Casa de Toño, the Mexican McDonald's. I love it and while its preparation has been completely industrialized, the flavors are still there. Plus, it's a good excuse to try other popular dishes if you get the small pozole or decide to share.

11. IT'S PRONOUNCED MOH-LAY

We're not quite finished with food for the Gods yet so hold on. *Mole* (pronounced moh-lay, not "mole" like the dark skin spots) was a traditional Aztec dish only offered to the gods, priests, and royalty when it contained chocolate. Chocolate was sacred for the Aztecs, so only the privileged could consume it. Fortunately, the consumption of chocolate is no longer discriminatory and not all moles contain it either.

Mole is a paste made from ground chilis, spices, and sometimes chocolate. The paste is then diluted with broth until it becomes a sauce that can be poured over chicken, pork, or tortillas. It also comes in every color of the rainbow except blue and purple, so I can almost bet you'll find one you like. While they are all good, I suggest trying the brown/black varieties because they're the most traditional.

When you do order it though, make sure to ask the waitress if it has any chocolate. Many people dislike the added sweetness that comes from it so most restaurants opt to leave it out. Nonetheless, I think, if prepared right, the chocolate brings out the spices and chilis a lot more. Luckily, finding a restaurant that serves good mole is not as hard as finding an Aztec god. You can find the dish in most Mexican restaurants, but you can never go wrong ordering mole at El Cardenal.

12. TO MAKE IT SPICY OR NOT SPICY?

All this talk about the ingredients in mole got me thinking about dried chilis. Their redness, spice, the depth of flavor they add to any preparation. All this leads me to our next dish: *caldo tlalpeño*. This typical Mexican dish is made from chicken and vegetable soup that's been seasoned with chipotle, making it a slightly spicier version of your average chicken soup.

Some people claim that the chipotle should only really tint the soup, while others argue that it should have enough presence in it to make it spicy. I agree with the latter, because every element in a dish should add something to the overall flavor. Whatever the case should be though, the only thing we all agree on is that caldo tlapeño needs chipotle, be it for color or spice.

Common vegetables include chopped carrots, green pumpkin, and potatoes. Several restaurants also serve it with a bit of white rice and chickpeas, which I think add a wonderful creaminess to the dish. While the preparation is not hard itself, proper seasoning is required to elevate it from an ordinary soup to one you will never forget! The combination of ingredients and flavors also happen to make it an amazing comfort dish, perfect for cold, rainy days.

Caldo tlalpeño can be found in most Mexican restaurants, but I highly recommend those found in small *fonditas* (small traditional eateries). Unfortunately, fonditas are not as common in the city as they are elsewhere in the country, but you might come across one in the more artsy districts like Condesa, Nápoles, or Roma. In case you can't find one, I suggest the following restaurant chain: Toks. It's the American equivalent of Denny's and the British Garfunkel's.

13. YOU'RE NOT ALL HOT STUFF

I've had enough hot food for now, so let's talk about ice cream. Ice cream is called *helado* (translates to "frozen") in Mexico City, but is referred to as *nieve* ("snow") pretty much everywhere else. It is the perfect snack for the city's hot summer days, but apparently there is a big difference between what people understand from helado and nieve so beware.

To me, it has always been nieve but *chilangos* (someone from the city) are quick to correct you. Thus, a seemingly obvious difference is pointed out and a very illogical explanation is offered up every time I go get ice cream. Anyhow, helado is the term used for both cream and water-based ice cream here. I won't go into the cream-based ones because it's the water-based ones that drive me nuts! If you've tried fruta enchilada (tip 5), you'll understand how much Mexicans love fresh fruit, so when I say water-based ice cream just imagine all your favorite fruits turned into a frozen treat.

Popular flavors include tamarind, passionfruit, and lemon with a bit of dried chili and chamoy. Unfortunately, not all ice cream is created equal. While I think most ice cream found in carts outside museums and in public parks is okay, I would not go out on a limb and say much more than that. It's just okay but it tends to be over-sweetened and that's a big no-no for me. All this is not to discourage you from giving it a try, especially if it's boiling hot, but if you want the full experience give these a try: Chiandonis, Amorino, and Ola Malú.

14. ALL YOU KNEAD IS LOAF

If you're not big on ice cream though, don't worry! Not all is lost. Yet. We've still got *pan dulce* (sweet bread, similar to danish pastries) to redeem you. Pan dulce refers to a variety of sweet breads. It's an important part of our culture and cannot be absent at the breakfast table. There are about as many sweet breads as there are stars in the galaxy, so we'll only cover the basics.

Our first contestant for a place at the breakfast table is the *concha*. We touched upon conchas in tip 9 but, basically, they are sweetened buns covered with a thin layer of crumbly goodness! Actually, they are a lot like the Japanese melonpan. Traditional flavors include vanilla and chocolate. However, more "millennial" flavors are becoming increasingly popular too. More gourmet bakeries will probably have red velvet, matcha, and hibiscus versions as well as seasonal varieties. Served warm, these have to be everyone's favorite!

15. A LOVER'S TREAT

Besos are next on our list. The name of these sweet treats translates to "kisses" because of the puckered up shape of two small buns joined together by fruit jam. Think of the buns as two muffin tops cut off and joined by strawberry or apricot jam in the middle. Is it the love or jam that binds them together? Does any couple really know the answer to this question?

If the cute name is not enough for you, besos also happen to be covered in sugar. Altogether, these desserts look like sugary jam clouds on dull plastic trays. Unfortunately, I haven't bought into their romantic side yet... In fact, I would dare say most people who eat them are either single or recovering from a broken heart. Nonetheless, besos are absolutely loved so here we are. I'm not head over heels for these like I am for conchas, but I've got nothing against them as long as they spread the love. Who knows, Cupid might strike you with his arrow when you try one? Take your chances and find out.

16. WE'RE NOT HERE FOR SPAGHETTI

We really are not here for spaghetti, but *garibaldis*. No, not Giuseppe Garibaldi. Well, sort of. This pan dulce was named after the Italian general because of its creator's admiration of Garibaldi, but his personality does not live up to its taste. Garibaldis are meant to be delicate and sweet, bathed in a thin layer of apricot jam, and then covered with round white sprinkles or the fancy nonpareils. Saying nonpareils has always sounded a little snobby for me, I'm sorry!

Anyhow, this baked good, in my opinion, looks a little bit funny, but tastes surprisingly good (or so they say). I'm still not sold on these just because the sprinkles are too sweet for me. I'm not allowed to say much since it's my husband's favorite, but I'll live with that. There are worse things than upside-down cupcakes covered in sprinkles sitting on your kitchen table, right?

17. GRAVEYARD PICNICS

Some of you probably travelled a long way for cupcakes with sprinkles. If that's the case, you're lucky I've got a special treat for you. *Pan de muerto* (bread of the dead) is a traditional bread eaten on the Day of the Dead, on November 1st. If you're not sure what kind of celebration this is, think of the parade in the Spectre 007 movie. That's Day of the Dead: a parade full of *catrinas* (dolled up skeletons), a visit to the cemetery, and lots of yummy food.

It's a beautiful celebration that's being lost to Halloween, but at least it looks like pan de muerto is not going anywhere. It is round, tastes a bit like orange, and is covered in sugar. While you can find it on most breakfast tables around the time of year, it is typically placed in an altar alongside portraits of our loved and lost.

Legend has it that November 1st is the only day of the year when the dead can rise from their graves and visit the living. In preparation, everything is already set out, ready for their arrival with a warm meal. Family picnics at the graveyard on this day are not uncommon either.

Luckily, you can find this bread without necessarily summoning the dead. Although it's

33

considered the specialty treat of November 1st, let's face it, no one is going to wait around the whole year to only taste this once. As a result, it's become much more common to find pan de muerto from October to mid-November. After that, the craze usually starts to die down in preparation for the next baked good we'll discuss.

18. CROWN JEWELS

Hold up, we're still in Mexico so the only crown jewels you'll hear about here are those on the crowns of the Wise Men. As you may or may not know, Mexico is a very religious country, with Catholicism ingrained into our culture left and right. While religious persecution isn't an issue here, Catholicism is very important so don't be surprised to find pictures of saints inside an Uber or religious figurines near the cash register at a restaurant. Despite this, don't feel indoctrinated. Most Mexicans are laid-back even when it comes to religion. Having said this, let's get on to our next dessert: *rosca de reyes* (the kings' bread).

The rosca de reyes is a bread roll shaped like a ring that is decorated with fresh fruits, a sweet crumbly paste, and a traditional guava or quince candy called *ate* (pronounced ah-tay). Originally, it was also stuffed with a tiny porcelain doll of Jesus Christ and the person who found it upon eating the bread was given good luck for the entire year. In recent years, the excitement of finding the porcelain doll has evolved into hiding up to ten dolls in each rosca de reyes. Some people argue that this is straying from tradition, especially with the recent craze for Star Wars-themed roscas with a Baby Yoda hidden inside. I honestly don't mind the theme or how many dolls are inside as long as it's reason enough for a family gathering.

Anyway, the rosca de reyes is usually very colorful and is topped with figs, maraschino cherries, almonds, etc. These decorations are meant to resemble the jewels in the Wise Men's crowns when they found baby Jesus. If you're not sure what to expect from this bread, think of a sweet ovaled bagel with lots of sweet toppings. Yes, that sounds about right!

Supposedly, it's only eaten on January 6th but we've found our way around that too by selling it from the start of December. However, finding a doll does not come without its responsibility. It will bring good luck, but it will also present you with the commitment of organizing the next religious family gathering. What does this mean? You will make the *tamales* for the next celebration and that's not exactly an easy task.

19. HOT TAMALES? YES AND NO

Any American reading this will be thinking of the iconic cinnamon-flavored candy called Hot Tamales. Trust me, this is not what we're here for. Those Hot Tamales are far from our hot tamales, which are a very traditional dish with many variations. Tamales are made from dough filled with mole, pork rind, etc. Then, they are steamed in a corn husk or banana leaf until fully cooked. Making them is not as easy as it sounds. If you were excited about finding one of the dolls hidden in the rosca de reyes, February 2nd is around the time you start wishing you hadn't.

The tradition in Mexico is that finding a doll in a rosca means having to make the tamales for the family-gathering on Candlemas Day. Fortunately for most of us, February 2nd is like an unofficial National Tamales Day. They're everywhere so none of us have to worry about making them ourselves. As a trained chef, I say this with a kind of merry guilt. I love tamales and I always made them with my grandma, so I know homemade ones are the real deal. But recently, the thought of sticking my hands into hot dough (never a good idea) and then making hundreds of them does not exactly make me jump with excitement. At least not when I'm busy preparing several cakes a day. Hopefully, I will come around soon enough though.

Even better is that tamales are available year round, in the mornings. I don't know what to call these early-morning gods or if there's even a name for them, but there are people whose job is to make tamales and then ride around in their bicycle carts selling them to the beautiful and damned. Make sure to start searching for a cart early in the day, or better yet, ask a local if they know where to find tamales nearby. If you're unsure about walking up to a stranger, just ask the hotel staff. I can guarantee you the receptionists, security guards, porters, or cleaning staff will know of at least one good one. And they're ridiculously cheap as well, the average tamal can cost anywhere from $15 to $30 pesos ($0.75-$1.5 USD). Tamales do not discriminate.

20. ON STEROIDS

If tamales were on steroids, *guajolotas* would be it. The guajolota is a sandwich that's filled with a tamal of your choice and topped with cream and/or salsa. It is amazing! Fortunately, you don't have to go very far to get one of these if you're already at a cart that sells tamales. Both guajolotas and tamales are often sold in the same place because they share a bloodline.

A lot of people have heart attacks just thinking about all the carbohydrates in guajolotas. I don't blame them. I was one of its biggest sceptics but I've since been converted. However, I definitely would not recommend it without the salsa or cream because I think they would be too dry. Also, make sure to have a drink handy. The people who sell tamales can help with that because they also come prepared with drinks.

21. READ THE INSTRUCTIONS OR ELSE

If dough on dough wasn't enough already, you're probably going to have to swallow everything with the help of an *atole*. Atole (pronounced ah-toh-lay) is a warm prehispanic beverage made with cornstarch.

Originally, it also contained honey and chili, but we've moved away from that and into the world of milk, *piloncillo* (a type of brown sugar), and vanilla.

Thanks to the wonders of the modern era, we do not need to wander deep into jungles to find indigeneous communities who still make this traditional drink. Atole is a beloved breakfast drink, making it easy to find with tamales. I promise you 95% of the time the people who sell tamales will have a big jug of atole too. However, make sure to get it early in the morning because it finishes pretty quickly. The mornings in Mexico City tend to be very chilly so workers often load up on this warm drink on their way to work.

If you're not lucky enough to still find some in the cart, don't worry! You can also find instant versions of it in the supermarket, sold in small packets with serving sizes for armies. Make sure to read the packet instructions because if you don't, you will have atole for weeks. Reading the instructions is as hard as it gets, though. The preparation is pretty simple. All you need to do is heat a little bit of milk and dissolve part of the powder into it. Once it's well dissolved, add the rest. If you do not follow my exact steps you will end up with a lumpy liquid that's neither atole nor anything known to man.

22. YOU'VE SPILT TOO MUCH MILK

Speaking of the dangers of not following instructions, *champurrado* has come to mind. Champurrado is also a warm prehispanic drink, except this one was used as part of Aztec rituals and ceremonies. You did not want to disrespect the gods in the presence of this drink...

Anyhow, champurrado is made from *masa* (corn tortilla dough) diluted in water, cacao beans, and cinnamon. Over time, we've considerably sped up this process by using powdered cocoa and cinnamon instead of the raw beans and sticks. It's a lot like atole but if you're unsure of the differences, here are the main ones: it's made from diluted dough and it tastes like chocolate.

What does it look like? From my experience in baking, it looks like accidentally spilling too much milk on a cupcake batter and then intentionally mixing it. That sounds about right. It has that not-quite-dough consistency but it's still thick like honey or caramel. Like atole, this is also enjoyed with tamales. However, I recommend sharing the drink with your loved one or a family member because it is extremely filling (it is watered-down dough, after all!). It's good but between tamales and champurrado, I'd rather have more tamales. You know, something that's actually food.

23. LEARN TO SAY NO

I'm not much of a coffee gal, but if you enjoy it, you need to try *café de olla*. Most people go crazy for it, but I just go crazy because of it. Café de olla is coffee that's spiced and brewed in an earthen clay pot. Beside the special flavor that the pot gives it, the coffee is spiced with cloves, star anise, and orange zest. It's not that I don't think it sounds amazing, I do... but coffee is my kryptonite.

About two birthdays ago, I remember we were home and I had just sliced my apple pie. Yes, I'm that type of person. I don't like birthday cake, so I make apple pie or whatever else I fancy on my birthday. Anyway, someone had prepared some coffee and I accepted a small cup out of embarrassment to admit that I don't like or drink coffee. There I was, pretending to sip twice, actually drinking a tiny bit once, pretending to sip twice, actually drinking once...

Everything seemed okay until it wasn't. My heart was racing, my hands were shaking, and I could feel control of my facial muscles slipping away into numbness. Could this be the end of me? No. It was the end of me ever accepting any coffee again, so something good came out of it. It's a real treat, just not so much my kind of treat.

However, it's a rather special treat so you may have to hunt it down a little among several Mexican food establishments. It's not difficult to make, but the amount of clay pots a restaurant might need to have in order to offer it is apparently not worth it. Good places to look for it, according to the world's biggest fan of café de olla (AKA my husband), are small family-owned restaurants. And also restaurants along highways, but you won't find any of those inside the city.

24. STUFF YOURSELF

Speaking of things that are hard to find, it seems like somewhere along this book I decided to bring you along for a year's worth of limited edition Mexican food. This was not planned, I promise. *Chiles en nogada* are large poblano chilis stuffed with *picadillo* (minced meat with vegetables or dried fruits), topped with a light and airy cream and bits of pomegranate for added freshness. More specifically, this is the only thing you should ever stuff yourself with.

Chiles en nogada don't necessarily sound like it but they are a true delicacy. They're also an acquired taste for some, so much that I would dare say it's a 50/50 chance a Mexican might like it. By no means does this "reveal" that it's bad, it's just like the brownie dilemma; some prefer it cakey and others like it fudgy. It's the same for chiles en nogada, but we're not discussing cakey or fudgy here. The thing with this dish is that some people can't wrap themselves around a sweet main course. Because, if you haven't noticed, we almost don't like chili.

Don't get me wrong, this was not a love-at-first-sight story for me! I inherited a rejection for them from my family, so I unquestioningly dismissed them until I met my husband. They're one of his favorite dishes and he raved about them long and hard. As much as I wanted to share his excitement, I couldn't. But there wasn't a real reason for my dislike, you know what I mean? Anyway, it got to a point where I had heard so much about these chiles en nogada that they piqued my curiosity. Unfortunately, the season had passed and I could not do more than fantasize about them for another eight months or so.

When they were available again, I really tried not to like them but there was no denying they were good. And so, I was hooked.

If you're here during the summer months, make sure to give one a try. Not all chiles en nogada are good because they are difficult to make, but I highly recommend those found in Toks or YUG. The latter is vegetarian, but they're that good.

25. OOEY-GOOEY AND DELICIOUS

If you were intrigued by the previous dish but are unsure whether you'll like the combination, try *chiles rellenos*. These are the baby brothers of chiles en nogada. They're completely savory and, unlike chiles en nogada, are dipped in a light batter and then deep fried.

Some chiles rellenos (stuffed chilis) are filled with cheese, others with beans, and if you're really lucky, with picadillo. While I absolutely love and adore them, the ones with cheese or picadillo are the best ones. Fortunately, these are not too hard to find. Almost any popular Mexican restaurant, like El Cardenal or Toks, will have them year-round.

You may want to proceed with a little caution at first because while the type of chili used to make them tends to be sweet, you can occasionally stumble upon a spicy one. It's not a level of spicy you'll cry over but you may need more than one glass of water to get over that relationship.

If you happen to get them freshly made at a market, ask for tortillas and a side of *arroz rojo* (red rice) to go with it. Then, prepare to feast on the most delicious tacos ever! It's not rocket science, just fill your tortilla with some red rice and add your chili. It's a match made in heaven! Let it cool enough so that you don't burn yourself with the hot oil, but not so much that any cheese inside stiffens. You want it to be ooey-gooey and delicious! Nothing on Earth is more delicious (this is one of my favorite dishes ever!), but if it happens to be too spicy for you, don't worry. An ice-cold glass of an *agua fresca* will bring you back to life in no time.

26. AGUA FRESCA

When you're looking for something refreshing, something to really quench your thirst, grab a glass of an *agua fresca*. It's not a particular beverage, it just refs to a variety of flavored waters. Popular flavors include *jamaica* and *horchata*.

Jamaica refers to a drink made from dried hibiscus flowers that have been steeped in hot water and sweetened with sugar. Sometimes the kind you find in restaurants is overly sweet or made with an artificial syrup. If it's too sweet just add more water. There isn't much of a solution to artificial flavoring, though. If you're unlucky enough to have this be your first experience with jamaica, don't give up! I promise it's worth it. A cold glass of *jamaica* is one of my favorite drinks in the world! It's sweet and tangy, and has so much depth it almost feels creamy? Maybe that's just me.

The next drink I will discuss is one I don't like: horchata. No, I'm not recommending you try something bad, it's just I don't like it. I don't enjoy creamy beverages that are advertised as refreshing. May creamy and refreshing never find world peace. I hate the combination that much. However, I find myself undoubtedly recommending this because I have never met another person who does not love it.

Horchata is a traditional drink made from rice, milk, vanilla, cinnamon, and sugar. It's everything I would expect from a rice pudding but not a drink. To me, it just feels like a liquid dessert but for that I'd rather eat melted ice cream. Either way, horchata is hands-down the preferred agua fresca by most Mexicans. That's just strange to me, but I'm not about to start questioning life.

If you're looking to try both, you're in luck! Where there is jamaica there is horchata, I swear. I'd never given it much thought but it's true. You can find both aguas frescas in restaurants, markets, and street-side food stalls. Perhaps not Oxxo's (the Mexican equivalent of a 7-Eleven or Spar), but other than that you could probably get them on the moon too.

27. WHERE'S THE LETTUCE?

Let's face it, Mexico isn't exactly the ideal foodie travel destination for vegans or vegetarians. We're still exploring those diets like Curiosity is Mars (and I imagine the rover knows more). Our cuisine is heavily meat-based, especially with our history of hard labor since colonial times. Consequently, plant-based anything isn't our national anthem. It's quite the opposite. Most people look for filling meals packed with protein and carbs to get them through the day instead of salads or veggie roasts.

The typical response to claiming you're a vegan or vegetarian here is a wide-eyed look followed by a confused laugh and a question like "can you eat fish?". Up until around five years ago, you could not even find any vegan or vegetarian alternatives to everyday products in the supermarket. Fortunately, the food scene has changed and these diets are beginning to enter the market. Slowly but surely.

My job here is to save the day and say that although our diet is meat-based, it's not impossible or too hard to find something vegetarian (vegan is harder, I admit). We eat a lot of beans and potatoes, for example, so you can always order some bean or potato flautas or *quesadillas* (like tacos with different fillings). Some places even have delicious *flautas de jamaica* (deep-fried hibiscus tacos) or soy-based *tacos al pastor* (a marinated-meat taco), so even if you happen to be the Cheerio in our world of Fruit Loops you will not starve. Promise.

However, you may want to ask what the beans or potatoes were fried in, because they happen to be plant-based but it's not intentional, which means they're likely to have been fried in pig's lard if you're not careful.

Anyway, here are some good vegetarian/vegan restaurants where you won't have to double guess your every bite: YUG, Pandora, and Plantasia.

28. MY NORTH STAR

I think I may have overdosed on nutrients because of the previous tip, so let's go back to the really good stuff. All of the fat and unhealthy we avoided before is rushing to us right now, and this time with more crunchy, deep-fried goodness than ever. Pork rind tacos. These are not just any rind tacos, they are Monterrey-style. These are my favorite tacos and they will be yours too.

Forget the fitness considerations, it's not time to be counting calories! I guess now would be the time to disclose these tacos are not even remotely healthy. It's deep fried pork rind with a little bit of meat, just enough so you get a little bit of a soft consistency in all the crunchy goodness! Plus, they are topped with brined bell peppers, purple onion, and chili. If that's not enough, they also throw in some avocado and bring over about six types of salsas for you to add to your heart's content. They're not small either; most people fill up with two. I like to eat 4, just for the sake of it. We live relatively far so I must load up every time we go. My birthday is the happiest time of the year because I don't need an excuse to drive all the way down there, we can go just because.

Unfortunately, *tacos de chicharrón norteño* are not a thing in Mexico City. Few people know them and far less businesses prepare them. Lucky for you, I've gone through the trouble (my husband has, actually) of finding the only ones you'll ever need: Tacos Orinoco. They also open late into the night so you don't need to worry too much about whether they'll be open or not. However, be ready to find a line during peak hours. Not huge, but some. Once you try them though, be ready to follow them to the end of the world!

29. ALL YOU NEED IS LOVE AND *TLACOYOS*

This deep-fried love story is not over yet. Now, we're onto *tlacoyos*: a deep fried dough patty that's been mixed with a filling like cheese, potato, or beans. Then, it's topped with a small portion of a casserole like *chorizo con papas* (chorizo cooked with potatoes), picadillo, etc. Finally, it's served warm with chopped lettuce, cream, cheese, and a salsa of your choice.

If you really imagine them, and hallucinate a little, they're like savory English biscuits or scones, except with a bunch of toppings and without the crumbliness. If you like flautas, chances are you will like tlacoyos too. There's really not a lot of science to them, but finding a good tlacoyo isn't easy. Perhaps the dough isn't the difficult thing about them but delicious casseroles and salsas to top them with are harder to come by than it seems. It's almost like finding a good burger or pizza, you know? Most of them are alright, but a really good one is hard to find. So pop over to the nearest streetside market and start hunting some down! Streetside markets are usually found in touristy areas during the weekends from around 9:00 am to 1:00 pm. Tlacoyos are a delicious breakfast, so pass on the pancakes for once, I promise you it'll be worth it.

30. WE WEREN'T SPEAKING OF PANCAKES

Indeed we were not speaking of pancakes in the previous tip but bringing them up actually made me think of sweet breakfast foods like crepes. Mexico City is no Paris, but we do have some pretty killer crepes. Savory and sweet, there is bound to be a combination you've never seen before.

Like with everything else, we have added our Mexican touch to them and even came up with wacky combinations. For example, crepes filled with *cajeta* (a caramel-like substance made from burnt goat's milk) or *rajas poblanas* (a sliced chili that's been cooked with corn and mixed with a creamy sauce). I understand you didn't come here for crepes but I do understand those random afternoon cravings. Luckily, crepes are a popular snack so you will probably find them in many shopping malls or street-side stalls, but the best ones in the city are found in La Creperie de la Paix and Cluny's. Both of these establishments are known for some of the best crepes around, so don't just take my word for it!

In my completely biased opinion, I'm going to go ahead and say Cluny's is better just because the cozy little restaurant holds sentimental value to me. It's a place my husband and I visited on several occasions before getting married. In other words, if you're looking to pop the question, Cluny's should be your one and only.

31. CHURR' ALL I NEED

Sometimes we're not speaking but you're all I need. No, not my husband. Churros! And we unfortunately don't speak much because they're far from where I live. The peace and quiet from living in the suburbs comes with a price, not being able to get to my favorite places within minutes. I'm still deciding if it's worth it, not necessarily because of the churros but they're on my list.

You've probably had this sweet treat elsewhere, especially if you've been to Spain, but Mexican churros are better. Isn't everything? I'm not bothering with discussing the origin of churros because Mexicans say they're Mexican, Spaniards will say they're from Spain, and some people even trace them back to China! Potato potahto, if they're good count me in!

The basic ones are served hot and sprinkled with sugar and cinnamon, but it starts to get a little crazy from there. You can get them filled with fruit jam or compote, cream cheese, *cajeta*, or get a bunch of dipping sauces. One place has even mastered churro ice-cream sandwiches, *El Moro*. This business was brought to Mexico by a Spaniard in 1933 when he moved to the city and noticed nobody sold churros.

Since then, *El Moro* has become one of the most loved and traditional places to eat churros.

Their menu now includes ice cream, milkshakes, and *tortas* (a type of sandwich). Between the churros and *tortas*, I prefer the latter but that's not to say I don't enjoy churros on chilly afternoons. It just depends on what I'm craving. To my surprise, they also have at least one vegan option for everything on their menu, so who needs lettuce anyway?

32. WE ALL PACK A BOOK WE WON'T READ

Save yourself the trouble and leave out any books you're trying to convince yourself you'll have time to read. You won't. Mexico is too spectacular. No quiet nights for reading are available here. That doesn't mean you'll be out partying every day, but more like exploring or having dinner late into the night. By the time you return to your hotel, all you'll think about is showering and planning tomorrow's meals.

However, that doesn't mean that you can't surround yourself with some good books and a meal while you're here. Mexican (and Latin American)

literature is some of the most underrated i
but we're full of national treasures like Juan
José Emilio Pachecho, and Octavio Paz. Instead of
wasting precious space on books you were already
reading, you can thank me later for giving you the
opportunity to purchase books that will not find
anywhere else.

If you enjoy visiting libraries during your
travels, I highly recommend *El Péndulo*. This is a
library like no other, and if you Pinterest enough (like
me) you'll find it among the ten most beautiful
libraries in the world! Don't expect a majestic library
as old as time like German ones, though. *El Péndulo*
is definitely modern and reflects a kind of intellectual
urban-jungle vibe. At least the one in Polanco does
(that's the one in the top 10 so go there!).

While you browse, you can order drinks (even
wine!) and grab a bite at the café inside. The food is
surprisingly good and the names of the dishes are sure
to put a smile on your face. They have the Chicken
Neruda Salad and Salad of Solitude, for example.
You can't really go wrong with what you order, the
food actually lives up to Da Vinci's and Foucault's
reputation.

33. POUR DECISIONS

Forgive my bad puns (which I love), but this is an invitation for drinks. Definitely not one in which you can make poor decisions, though. I'll explain later. Anyway, something about drinking wine and reading makes me picture myself in a beautiful cocktail gown sipping wine while reading. The reality is far from that; me in pajamas on my third day without showering, my hair in a less-than-sexy messy bun, reading upside down on the sofa, with an empty wine glass that's just there to keep me company. My hubby just stares at the accumulation of stains on my t-shirt and my still-empty pages of pure genius can only sigh. Writing can be difficult. If this is also you or you're just looking for an excuse to actually dress up, my next recommendation could not come at a better time. Now that I think about it, it actually would not be a bad idea for me to dress up and go out.

The *San Ángel Inn* is one of the most famous restaurants in town. The place is a seventeenth century colonial estate that's been accommodated as a restaurant since 1963. Today, you can still admire the original architecture. Its beautiful central patio and majestic halls evoke elegance all around. Yes, this is a fancy restaurant. Not fancy like "book a table one year in advance", but fancy enough for there to be a dress code and a reservation of possibly two or more days in advance.

I'm not talking about an all-inclusive beach-resort-restaurant dress code where you can practically show up in a bikini but no flip-flops and that'll do. They mean it here. You don't need to go all Beyoncé-at-the-Met-Gala, but you will need a dress shirt and a blazer or a nice dress. No sweatshirts, pajamas, or t-shirts.

Once you get past the dress test, the food is supposed to be amazing. Entire generations rave over this restaurant, but I can only imagine why because I've never gotten in and stayed. This sounds like an escape from prison, but no. In my defense, I've only gone there once but it wasn't exactly a pleasant experience. I was greeted at the entrance by a very evident impolite frown, but we were then seated at our table.

An army of waiters arrived and put more plates and cutlery on the table than we have in our crockery. It was too much so we kindly asked them to remove everything because we would not order a main but more like wine and dessert. Our honesty was greeted by crude glares.

Suddenly, the army of waiters disappeared and gathered against the wall in a very obvious chit-chat. Eventually, the head waiter came over and began making excuses as to why they couldn't serve us, and very rudely pointed out my clothes as one of those reasons. My husband argued with them for a couple minutes until they agreed to serve us, but it was more like they were doing us a favor so we got up and left. That's right folks, my "pour decision" was not getting tipsy on wine, it was my choice of clothes and not spending hundreds of pesos on a 3-course dinner each.

Sadly but proudly, we have never gone back. I say this with a certain regret because the previous head waiter happened to be my Uber driver on one occasion and he spoke wonders of the place. Apparently, he'd worked at San Ángel Inn for over eighteen years and retired just one month before. He gave me a long list of dishes (some that were only prepared upon request) and said that if I ever visited the restaurant, I should tell the waiter we were friends. The experience with this polite head-waiter-gone-rogue set the bar high for me, but ultimately set me up for disappointment too.

By the time my husband and I actually went to the restaurant, I could neither remember his name nor all the dishes he had recommended. It wouldn't have mattered, though. Nothing could have saved us from the awful service and snobby waiters, not even a life's dedication to the place. Which is a shame because the restaurant is absolutely gorgeous and the food's supposedly amazing, but my impression of the place has been bitterly tainted.

Don't let my experience keep you from giving the restaurant a shot. Perhaps I just happened to be the unlucky customer who showed up on a bad day? I don't know. I'm just being brutally honest. At least now you'll know what to expect. The only other thing I can say is, if you're brave enough to go there, order the strawberry jubilee. They're not on the menu, but they're the only thing I can remember from my conversation with the old man.

34. NOT A SUN MAID GIRL

I admit I got a little bit upset from remembering that humiliating evening, so I want to cheer the (my) mood by talking about *alegrías*, a typical Mexican candy. The name alegrías means "happiness" in English, so there was no better way to brighten the mood than these! Interestingly enough, they do bring out a lot of smiles too.

Alegrías are made from puffed amaranth seeds stuck together with honey or a sugary syrup (the best ones are made with honey). These usually come in the shape of a rectangle or circle and are individually packaged for easy transport. They are the right amount of sweet and interestingly crunchy. I feel intrigued every time I have them because they're not crunchy per se, maybe it's just the sensation you get from breaking off the amaranth?

To make them even better, sometimes they also come with toasted pecans, peanuts, and pumpkin seeds. Avoid the ones with raisins because, who likes raisins? Sorry, I'm not a Sun Maid girl.

35. COCONUTS ABOUT YOU

Now that I've recovered from my brief but unpleasant walk down memory lane (tip 33), I'm in the mood for more candy, except this one is not as healthy as a puffed amaranth bar. *Cocadas* are a typical Latin American candy that is very popular in Mexico. They are made from grated coconut, sugar, vanilla, and egg yolks.

Cocadas have an extremely rich flavor and they often even taste creamy. They come in white, orange, and even pink versions. I know the white ones lack the egg yolks, but I have no idea where the pink ones get their color from. Maybe they're flamingo poop? It's either that or food coloring.

They're very sticky so make sure to save part of the wrapping for you to hold on to them if you don't like getting your hands dirty, like me. Cocadas won't stick to your teeth like toffee but it'll definitely leave a very thick sugary covering on your fingers if you're not careful, and the sugar isn't finger-licking good. The coconut is, but that's not what sticks to your hands. The cool thing about cocadas is that you can find them, along with most typical candies, by parks. There will be people with wheel carts, baskets, or even blankets on the floor, with a wide array of typical candies. Sometimes the hygiene is dubious so try not to think too much about it. If it looks that bad, please walk away, better days and candy will come.

36. WORTH A SHOT

A lot of our snacks come with a certain leap of faith because they're out in the open and dust is likely to have fallen on it, but it's not always the case with *borrachitos*. Borrachitos are small pillows of tipsy and fun. Perhaps I exaggerated a little, you will not get tipsy on these (I think?) but they do contain liquor. Borrachitos are another flour-based treat on our list so I hope that none of you are on diets. If you are, Mexico is always a good place to break it! Besides, I doubt you'll be able to maintain it for long before giving in to our food.

They're made from flour, sugar, liquor, and all your favorite flavors. I'm not sure how, but the combination of these ingredients actually makes a creamy center that's very addictive. Popular flavors include strawberry, pineapple, and *rompope* (eggnog), and they often come in small boxes of about two or three flavors.

These are some of my favorite candies so make sure to get at least two boxes because, I promise you, they'll be gone within minutes! People who don't like borrachitos don't know they come in small boxes, and all the best things do.

37.BREAKFAST AT TIFFANY'S

I've never actually seen a Tiffany's outside a shopping mall so don't get your hopes up, our idea of breakfast at Tiffany's is different. Get up early on a Saturday morning, put on some pants and sweatshirt, just enough to say you're dressed and half-way decent, and drive to the nearest *barbacoa* restaurant you know. Fine, maybe not the nearest but one that you like.

Barbacoa is a true delicacy that dates back to the prehispanic era. It is a cooking method that consists of digging a large hole in the ground and heating it with different woods and stones, and then wrapping the meat in plantain leaves. After, the wrapped meat is placed on top of the hot wood and stones and left to cook for hours in the covered hole.

There are different types of barbacoa but the best one is made of sheep, so make sure to look for some. If you're like me and don't like to struggle with taking things off the bone or any of the grease, you're in luck too! Most establishments will already remove the bones for you, but it's always good to double check. It's typically sold by weight depending on the part of the sheep it is and you can make your own tacos from it. However, sometimes individual tacos are also sold in case you're not up for the math. Don't think about it too much because barbacoa runs out quickly! Since it's typically only sold on Saturdays and Sundays, you will find the streets empty but the restaurants full. However, don't expect a fancy restaurant or something too put together. *Barbacoa* restaurants tend to be very simple and look half-way-through-construction. In fact, some of the people who sell it do it straight from their trucks and just put out a couple of tables and chairs.

I bet you were expecting a different breakfast at Tiffany's, huh? Here you will certainly not be staring down at designer items while you enjoy a delicious breakfast. You will be watching cars drive by and will be listening to the sweet sound of the butcher chopping away.

38. IT'S LIKE BARBECUE

Another Mexican dish that will have you visiting a place that looks like a butcher shop as much as it does a restaurant, is *carnitas*. Carnitas are a very fatty but delicious dish made from braised pork. The meat simmers for hours on end until it becomes extremely tender, a bit like barbacoa.

It's also eaten in the form of tacos so be prepared for a hearty breakfast. I would recommend these with fresh orange juice or something that's healthy to pump some energy back into you. Do not ignore my advice about the orange juice. You will need it if you expect to do something other than lay in your hotel room the rest of the day. Please listen to me.

Like barbacoa, carnitas are also typically sold only on the weekends. If you're in town for two or so weeks, I recommend trying barbacoa one weekend and carnitas the next. I wouldn't do both during one weekend just because of how fatty they are, plus all of the other carbs you'll eat from tamales and pan dulce. If you're not too worried about your diet or think you can handle it, go for it. I'm just saying because even Mexicans approach carnitas with certain caution. And if we approach something with caution, everyone else should with three times the amount.

My only tip to those of you courageous enough to take my advice with a grain of salt is, don't eat both tortillas on your tacos. They will only make you feel more sluggish, so please stick to one like God intended. Oh, and add a bunch of chopped coriander, onion, and salsa.

39. COOL AS A CUCUMBER

Two fatty tips in a row have made me feel really sluggish, plus, the weather is super hot, so I need to freshen down a little. The only way to do that is with a cold beer and some *aguachile*. Made with raw shrimp, scallops, or fish, it's the ultimate appetizer for hot summer days. If you can take the heat, that is.

Aguachile is raw seafood that's been marinated with lime juice, chili, coriander, onion, and cucumber. Sometimes the liquid is blended so that the flavors are even, but other times the different elements are crushed using a mortar. I prefer a blended sauce and scallops for aguachile, but that's just my preference, and not all restaurants can accommodate my every wish. I guess I can't be the head chef in every kitchen.

Although this is one of the best seafood dishes I can recommend you try, whatever you do, stay away from it if you can't tolerate high levels of spiciness. The name aguachile means "chili water" so don't trust me if you don't want to, but names don't lie. Some restaurants prepare it a lot spicier than others, others use different ingredients, but the thing with aguachile is you never know. If you're keen on giving this a try, please ask your waiter how spicy it is before you order, or if they can use less chili in the preparation, because this is one dish that will have you curling up within a couple of hours if you're not used to the acidity or heat.

I love this dish and could eat bucketfuls of it if I didn't know it might make me scream in pain within a couple of hours. About one year ago, I got gastritis and since then aguachile and I have been on a break.

40. BUTTERFLY FLY AWAY

Something that I luckily don't have to be on a break from, is the famous *pescado a la talla*. I've known it as *pescado zarandeado* my whole life but I didn't grow up in Mexico City, so I'm going to spare you the confusion and refer to it as *a la talla*.

This dish consists of a whole fish that's been cut open like a butterfly and slathered with a red chili paste and spices. It is typically grilled or braised to give it a smoky flavor which only adds to the flavor party. Usually, it comes with a side of rice or salad.

The fish is not spicy but it is spiced, mainly with *achiote*, so be ready for a spice punch. Achiote is a red condiment from the seeds of the achiote tree, native to tropical Latin America regions. It is used because of the color, flavor, and aroma it gives to food, much like saffron. I think it tastes tangy like an orange, sour like a tamarind, and a little bit earthy. It's an interesting flavor, but one that needs to be handled with care because too much of it means you will not get it out of your system for a couple days. Other than that, it is actually a very common spice. Especially in southern Mexican cuisine from the states of Yucatán and Chiapas, achiote is a pantry-staple.

41. CHRISTMAS MORNING

Next up, we have another traditional dish with achiote: the *mixiote*. In my opinion, this is one of the most funny looking dishes in our cuisine. Mixiotes are small pouches of pit-barbecued animal protein like pork, rabbit, or chicken. They are very juicy because of the salsas they are made with plus all of the juice that is released during cooking. The wrapper is a thin translucent film that comes from *maguey*, the plant that tequila comes from. It's not edible but it does give the dish an Etsy-vibe because it's usually tied together with twine.

Opening the mixiote is also like opening presents on Christmas morning, there's always an element of surprise. Perhaps the blend of chilis is different or maybe they put more achiote in it; each mixiote is unique, like you and me.

If you're feeling adventurous though, you can also find mixiotes made of deer, crocodile, and wild boar. I have not tried them (yet) but hopefully I will get a chance soon enough. I know of one place to get these exotic versions but I've been putting it off because I'm scared of the market's reputation for creepy and strange ingredients. Luckily, the sides tend to be normal even if you're eating kangaroo meat.

42. CHIP CHIP HOORAY!

Our next dish is a popular appetizer but depending on the toppings or size, it may justify being the main course. If that's the case, you may get a weird look from the waiter but never mind them. *Tostadas* are not as equally fabulous for everyone, but they are beautiful in my eyes.

Tostadas are round corn chips the size of tortillas. They're like giant Tostitos but way less salty and are actually made from tortillas. However, these are just the canvases for talented artists. The real magic happens when you begin layering flavors. Some of them will have beans, others will have *nopales* or picadillo. You can also get them with ceviche, *cochinita pibil* (a spiced pork dish), or shredded chicken. The best ones in the whole wide world are the last three so I highly recommend them.

Most people don't think twice about tostadas and they are often regarded as food for the lower classes. I don't care, though. What's not to love about a crunchy base topped with anything you can imagine? Plus, you can add shredded lettuce, cream, cheese, and salsas! They're simple, fresh, and you can eat many of them. More importantly, they're extremely delicious and affordable.

However, don't let them sit for too long! Tostadas become soggy quickly so my recommendation would be to order one, eat it, and then order the next. I know the temptation to order them all at once is big (I've been there), but take it from a person who loves tostadas, don't. Sure, the toppings will still taste the same but none of them will be tostadas once they get soggy. You won't even be able to pick them up and that sucks.

43. THE FAT ONES AND WOODLICE

As I mentioned in the previous tip, *cochinita pibil* is a popular topping for tostadas, but it can also be eaten on its own, in tacos, or as the filling for *gorditas*. The name gorditas means "the fat ones". They are made from dough and are like tortillas, except thicker and can be opened up and filled. I don't eat them much but it's one of the dishes I'm most fond of because of the childhood memories it brings.

When I was little, my mom and I used to go to the food court of a small shopping mall in Reynosa, the border-city I was born in, and we would order *gorditas de cochinita pibil*. Every single time. It was our thing, you know? I had no idea what it was but I never asked, until I did. One ordinary day, we were ordering our gorditas and I asked my mom what they were made of. She smiled and said *"cochinita"*. Four-year-old me had a tiny heart attack and let out a nervous laugh. I had confused cochinita (the dish) with the word *cochinilla* (woodlice, a small gray insect that curls up). The thought of it both confused and mesmerized me. It was also a little disgusting.

While the lady at the establishment continued preparing our food, a million thoughts crossed my mind, like why my mom would feed me woodlice. I thought I no longer had much of an appetite for my gorditas but then the lady rang the bell my worries disappeared. They tasted too good!

We walked to the nearest table and sat down. My mom bit into hers while I continued analyzing mine. I was intrigued by how the pulled pork texture was achieved but what amazed me even more was how many insects were needed to make one gordita! I imagined they had to be hundreds or thousands, or as high as I could count back then, which I imagine was like fifty. I bit into my gordita and enjoyed it probably more than ever before, but I had to know everything. I put it down and I remember asking my mom how much woodlice was needed to make gorditas. She smiled and said "many". Now that I think about it, I'm not sure if she always knew I was referring to woodlice and found it amusing that I thought we were eating insects or if she didn't pick up on the difference between the words. After all, a four year old doesn't exactly have the best diction or pronunciation.

If she did realize and just didn't correct me, I thank her because she gave me a lot to think about over the next few years (until I was nineteen) and one of the best memories I have with her.

Anyway, gorditas come with all sorts of fillings. Don't think woodlice is the only kind! Picadillo, beans, and eggs are also popular fillings. If you're brave enough to break the status quo, add cream, cheese, and salsa! Avocado slices too if you can find some. If others around you stare, who cares? It's your gordita, not theirs!

44. NOT PINTEREST-PERFECT

All this talk about tostadas and gorditas got me thinking about *antojerías*, small restaurants that only serve Mexican comfort foods like flautas, gorditas, and *enchiladas*. While pinterest has done a good job popularizing these, it's done a mediocre one of portraying the real thing. They could not be further from the truth. Thick and whitewashed tortillas? Shredded cheddar cheese on top? Salsa that only covers the center of the enchilada and looks more like ketchup than anything else? Make it stop! We use real corn tortillas, *cotija* cheese, and cover them in salsa like we're deep-frying a donut. The most important thing, unless you're eating at a restaurant, they will never look as nice. We've got to make these lies stop. I admit that styling food to make it look nice is not the end of the world, but the corruption of ingredients is something I cannot stand. Where else do you think Taco Bell came from?

Anyway, I will leave my case against cultural appropriation for later. Enchiladas are tortillas that have been folded in half (like tacos) or rolled (like flautas) and filled with shredded chicken, beef, or potatoes. While still in the pan, they are bathed in salsa, typically red or green. Sometimes you can get half and half, but it depends on the place. Either way, once the tortillas have softened up a little, they are served hot with a drizzle of cream, a sprinkling of cheese, and avocado slices. Interestingly enough too, enchiladas are served in threes just like flautas. You cannot get one, like you would get a taco. Maybe heating the salsa and everything is too messy for you to only get one? I wouldn't blame them if that's the case. Thinking about all the cleanup for one enchilada is a no-no, even in my kitchen.

However, these are not baked. Ever. The next time you see something claiming to be Mexican that is baked, believe me it's not. Using our ovens for anything other than pan dulce isn't part of our culture so don't be fooled. We've mastered our stoves, our salsas, and toppings, over hundreds of years, so let's just pay tribute to that.

45. LITTLE RED RIDING HOOD'S BASKET

Soft tortillas also reminded me of *tacos de canasta*. I have not seen too many of them in the city but if you ever see a person riding around with a basket in the back of their bike or motorcycle, you can almost bet it's tacos de canasta. Either that or pan dulce, but you can't really complain if it's one or the other, can you?

Tacos de canasta are small tacos with all kinds of different fillings like *tinga* (a kind of shredded chicken), cochinita pibil, beans, etc. They're then placed inside a basket lined with plastic, where they will soften up from the steam. The result is glorious. It's probably just an optical illusion but you never really fill up on these. I think I can eat around ten of them.

Now that I think about it, I have never actually seen these inside restaurants which means you'll have to do some soul-searching to find them. They're one of my favorite things in the world so just know they are highly recommended by the likes of me. By now, I think we're acquainted enough to know I wouldn't lie to you. Not after I've even recommended things I'm not a fan of but can accept most people do, just because I want you to have an authentic culinary experience.

Once you track down a bicycle or motorcycle with a basket, you're set for life. But make sure to start hunting early because these are breakfast tacos, and everyone will close in on them as soon as they've identified a basket. You're not the only one looking for love. If you see several basket-bearers though, go for the one with the most people eating by it. However, don't expect tables and chairs. I can imagine riding around with about three hundred tacos on the back of your bike is already difficult enough to take on tables and chairs too. It may not be the most comfortable thing in the world, but you'll have to eat standing and juggle your drink too. I've actually given up on standing. If you can do an Asian squat, this is the best use you'll give it. Heads up: people will stare.

46. GOING ALL "GORDON RAMSAY"

Tinga is a traditional topping for tostadas and filling for tacos de canasta. It is made with shredded chicken and a sauce made from tomatoes and chipotle. However, I must admit that it has never been part of my diet and I don't think I've ever even tried it. Similar to the brownie-dilemma we discussed early on, 50% of people will say it's bland and the other 50% will take a bullet for it. Apparently, people like me do not fit into that pie chart because presentation is not part of the conversation?

In my opinion, *tinga* is one of those things that does not always look the most appetizing. The preparation is a gray-area where sometimes it'll be too watery, the chicken is so shredded it looks like a cat's hairball, or it tastes too much like tomato. Just because I don't remember ever tasting *tinga*, it doesn't mean I haven't seen enough of it to judge it. Plus, I basically studied to be able to judge dishes without necessarily tasting them. As far as looks go, it's not always appetizing, but the nation-wide inconsistency is what really throws me off.

However, I am not against the dish itself. A well prepared tinga actually sounds like something

I'd love to put on tostadas. It should be juicy but not watery and with a consistency that doesn't look like a blended chicken smoothie, please. The only places I would recommend eating this at are El Cardenal and La Casa de Toño.

As I write this, I find myself questioning whether I should recommend tinga or not just because of all my criticism towards it, but I have decided to leave it here. This dish deserves a place here and on every list. It's one of the most typical Mexican dishes even if I don't love it. If it's not on the menu, I wouldn't go out of my way too much to try it, but it's worth it if you've already tried everything else on this list.

47. A-MAIZE-ING

We've almost reached the end of our adventure, so the next dishes are all some of my favorite things in the world. First, we have *pastel de elote* or *pan de elote*. This basically translates into corn cake or bread, and it's full of delicious goodness. It's made with eggs, condensed milk, butter, and yellow corn. Some recipes call for flour and others don't, it just depends on what kind of texture you like best: pudding-like or crumbly.

Pan de elote is as traditional as it gets. It's one of the most iconic Mexican desserts and a favorite across the country. Have some with a cup of coffee or a scoop of vanilla ice cream, and your afternoon dessert will be absolutely perfect.

Although I own a bakery, I am not much of a sweets-person. Quite the opposite, actually. Pastel de elote, however, has always managed to win me over. Fortunately, you can find it on the menu at most restaurants but I would go ahead and skip this because they'll give you a tiny serving of it. Just head straight to a bakery and see if they sell whole loaves of it. I suggest grabbing one or two and bringing them back to your hotel. They will be your new favorite night-time snack.

48. ONE THOUSAND AND ONE NIGHTS (OR TACOS)

For some reason, tacos *al pastor* always tend to be the cheapest on the menu. It's always intrigued me, but I can't complain because they're one of my favorite tacos so I can eat more of them. If I only get tacos al pastor, I probably eat seven or eight of these. In my defense (but I don't really want to defend myself), they are small. Before you judge me, go ahead and try them.

Unlike other tacos, these are made from pork. They are heavily spiced and marinated in a chili-based sauce, cooked on a vertical rotisserie with an open flame. However, the preparation for tacos al pastor is never small-scale. Huge amounts of raw marinated pork are placed on the rotisseries of thousands of *taquerías* (taco establishments) around noon every day. Throughout the day, the meat is cooked to tender perfection but the fire never stops. Once orders start rolling in, thin slices are cut off the *trompo* (the huge meat arrangement) and a new raw layer of pork meat is exposed for slow-cooking again.

Trompos are something restaurants like to show off so any self-respecting taquería will have theirs in full glory at the front of the restaurant, near a window where anyone can also visibly feast upon it. That's not all, though! Aside from the wonderfully seasoned meat, it is served with slices of fire-grilled pineapple. Topped with chopped coriander, onion, and a red salsa, tacos al pastor are a match made in heaven (or the Middle East).

Don't get me wrong, tacos al pastor are not Middle Eastern but the cooking method and spices are largely based on that of shawarmas brought over by Lebanese immigrants in the nineteenth century. Eventually, the spices were adjusted to include Mexican ingredients like chili and achiote, and over time they became everyone's favorite taco.

49. A FRENCH KISS

Just like tacos al pastor spread by word of mouth, tacos *de lengua* did too but quite literally. De lengua means "of tongue", so be ready for the French-kiss of tacos because these are as odd as they are delicious if you've never tried them (the tacos, not French-kissing).

Tongue tacos are held almost to a gourmet level elsewhere in the country, but for some reason Mexico City has not fallen in love with them yet. I'm hoping that day will come soon so they're not as expensive anymore. Tacos de lengua are the caviar of tacos. Crazy expensive in comparison to other kinds, but exquisite if you can appreciate them. Their texture isn't for everyone, though.

Stand in front of a mirror and stick out your tongue. Take a look at all the tiny bumps on it. Now, imagine the same thing but a thousand times larger and rougher because we're talking about a cow's tongue. While it's not like you'll be chewing shards of glass or anything like that, some people can't get past the texture which can sometimes be a combination of tender and leathery. I think it's one of those things that make tacos de lengua so unique.

My grandma occasionally made these tacos when I visited, except I rarely got to try anything but the leftovers. By the time I was back from work, my uncle and cousins had already stopped by and finished them. If I was lucky, I could piece together a taco from the leftovers in the bowl but it was worth it.

Anyway, I'm trying to think of something to compare tongue to because it's definitely not a BigMac. It's somewhere between baked tofu and roasted beef chuck. It's springy but once you bite it, you can see different layers of meat. Sometimes it's chopped in small squares and others it's sliced whole so you can see the shape of the tongue, but it's equally delicious. Add some chopped coriander, onion, and a green salsa, and in it goes! Even if you're not into trying "weird stuff" like beef tongue, trust me on this. I don't fancy eating liver, guts, or anything like that, but tacos de lengua have stolen my heart since I was five.

50. SAY CHEESE

Once again, we've divided the nation. Quesadillas. To the world, they are tortillas filled with cheese. In Mexico, it's not so simple. The only place in the world where quesadillas are something different is Mexico City; here, a tortilla filled with anything other than cheese is a quesadilla. It can be tinga, cochinita, mole, you name it! This has sparked a nationwide debate over what a quesadilla really is.

There are more people in the rest of the country than there are in Mexico City, that's a fact. Therefore, if all of them say a quesadilla strictly and exclusively contains cheese, Mexico City should listen. However, there is something a little bit defiant about the city when it comes to taking culinary suggestions. Hence, forums have been filled, podcasts have been made, and divorces have been caused. I am not kidding when I say that scholarly debates have been held and serious investigations carried out, all for the sake of proving the other side wrong. To be honest, this is something I'm okay with as long as there comes a day of peace in which all quesadillas are made of cheese and only cheese.

I have to say that I am completely biased on this one because for nineteen years I lived and travelled to places in Mexico where quesadillas have cheese, so once I moved to the city it seemed plain ridiculous to me that this was the only place where this was questioned. Some things are just not meant to be questioned. What is Mexico City trying to do, cause a national identity crisis?

Either way, before you vote me into office, let's talk about quesadillas in Mexico City. Here (and only here) they are like tacos but instead of meat, they are filled with any of the other dishes and casseroles we have discussed throughout this book. I've given you plenty to work with by now so I hope you're not sitting there, reading this, wondering what I'm talking about. I've got my eyes on you, and the city does too. Go ahead and eat a year's worth of mole, chiles rellenos, and cochinita pibil in quesadillas. You also get bonus points if they're handmade tortillas!

Mexico is the only place that gets these dishes right. No sour cream, no cheddar cheese, no weird canned beans. Just simple, natural ingredients. After this amazing culinary tour, I hope you feel more confident about your time in Mexico and taste our culture one dish at a time. I've given you all the best dishes to get you started but don't be afraid to explore on your own. Our food and flavors are rare and unique, like every person in this country.

OTHER RESOURCES:

Links to travel websites, useful phone numbers, apps, or maps of the area.

- https://www.visitmexico.com/en/ --------- for travel tips and advice
- https://www.chilango.com/ --------- for the best local tips on food and entertainment

READ OTHER BOOKS BY CZYK PUBLISHING

Eat Like a Local United States Cities & Towns

Eat Like a Local United States

Eat Like a Local- Oklahoma: Oklahoma Food Guide

Eat Like a Local- North Carolina: North Carolina Food Guide

Eat Like a Local- New York City: New York City Food Guide

Children's Book: Charlie the Cavalier Travels the World by Lisa Rusczyk

Eat Like a Local

Follow *Eat Like a Local on* Amazon.
Join our mailing list for new books

http://bit.ly/EatLikeaLocalbooks

CZYKPublishing.com

Printed in Great Britain
by Amazon